Precious Moments

Book
of
Manners
for Girls

Precious Moments® Book of Manners for Girls
Text by Janna Walkup
Published by Harvest House Publishers
Eugene, Oregon 97402

Precious Moments® Book of Manners for Girls
Text copyright © 2006 by Harvest House Publishers, Inc.
Eugene, OR 97402

ISBN-13: 978-0-7369-1525-0
ISBN-10: 0-7369-1525-7

Artwork copyright © 2006 Precious Moments, Inc. *Precious Moments* is a
registered trademark used by PMI Licensee, Harvest House Publishers.
All rights reserved worldwide.

Design & production by Koechel Peterson & Associates, Inc.
Minneapolis, MN

Printed in Hong Kong

06 07 08 09 10 11 12 13 / NG / 10 9 8 7 6 5 4 3 2 1

Contents

Manners Make Life Happy and Nice!

Do you like giving your mom great big hugs? Is playing dolls with your friends one of your favorite things to do? Does putting on a pretend tea party—complete with fancy hats and pretty teacups and yummy cookies—with your grandma sound like a delightful thing to do?

If you love to play and have fun with others, you'll love learning about and practicing your good manners!

Manners are the things we say and the way we live and play that help us show other people that we love and care about them. Everything you do—eating your breakfast, talking on the telephone to your grandparents, unwrapping presents on your birthday—is made sweeter when you use your best manners.

It's fun to use good manners with your family and your friends. It's even fun to play pretend good manners games with your dolls and stuffed animals! You can practice being polite and kind. You can practice using happy words and having a smiling face. You can practice taking turns and letting someone else go first.

Good manners come from a loving heart. Good manners let other people know that they are special to you. Good manners say, "I love you!"

My Talking Manners

SPEAKING TO PEOPLE BIG AND SMALL

Just a few short years ago you were probably saying your very first words—*mama* or *cup* or *cat* or *ball*. Now you know the right words for just about everything! And you're ready to learn the right words to say at the right times.

Meeting and Greeting

The first thing you need to know about good talking manners is how to say hello. When someone walks into a room, it's nice to stand up to greet them. Smile big and look right at the person with your happy face.

A handshake is a nice way to say, "I'm happy to meet you." If the person is already a good friend or someone you really love a lot, you can always give them a great big hug.

Always try to put a smile on your face when you talk. If someone says something that doesn't make sense, you can just say, "Excuse me?" or "Pardon me?"

Your very best talking manners will help you get to know all sorts of people—big and small, young and old, boys and girls. You never know who might end up being a really fun friend!

The Name Game

People really like it when you say their name. It makes them feel special! So say, "Hello, Auntie Barbara!" Or, "I'm so happy to see you, Emma!" You can even use a pet's name: "You look so cute today, Butterscotch!"

Instead of saying, "Hey," always say, "Hello!" or just a nice, friendly, "Hi!" or "Good morning!"

If you don't know someone's name, go ahead and tell them your own name. Then you can say, "What is your name?" They will be happy to tell you!

When you meet a grown-up, always call them by Miss, Mrs., or Mr. and their last name—Mr. Jones, Mrs. Pansy, Miss Bluebonnet—unless they ask you to please call them something else. Even if they want you to use their first name, it's a little more special to use a title with their name. You can call your ballet teacher Miss Hannah or your Sunday school teacher Miss Cornelia. It shows that you care about them. And sometimes grown-ups will return the favor and say Miss along with your name! That makes you feel really special—and like a very big girl!

9

Everyone's Important!

When you are with a group of children—in a classroom, at someone's house for a playgroup, at the park—it's very important that you are nice to everyone. Try to talk to all of the kids if you can, and never, ever whisper or tell secrets in front of someone else. That makes people feel left out and sad, and nobody likes to feel that way.

If you do feel like whispering or saying something that might make someone feel bad, it's better not to say anything at all. Remember our differences are what make us special!

Learning to Listen

When someone else is talking, be sure to let them finish what they're saying before you start to talk. It might sound kind of silly, but part of talking is *listening*. And good listeners make good friends!

If two people are talking and you *really* need to say something, just use your words to politely get their attention: "May I speak to you?" or "May I please tell you something?" And only do this if you *really* need to talk to them—if a great big dog is headed for your baby brother, for instance.

Until We Meet Again!

The final part of talking manners is what happens when you're ready to go. You say goodbye!

But you don't just say, "See ya!" or "Later!" and run off to play. You go up to the person you are saying goodbye to and use your nicest manners to say that you had fun: "Goodbye! I had a lot of fun playing with you!" Then you can give them a hug if they're a special friend.

My Kindness Manners

WORDS THAT
ARE SWEET

Did you know that certain words are "magic" words? Now, these words don't work exactly like fairytale wishes. You won't suddenly find yourself dressed like Cinderella after you say them. These words won't magically do the dishes or even brush your teeth for you. But they *do* make everyone around you happy. And when you use these "magic" words, they make *you* happy, too!

Please. Thank you. Excuse me. I'm sorry.

You can use these "magic" words when you need something, or when someone has done something nice for you, or when you made a mistake you wish you hadn't made. "Magic" words are like Band-Aids that make everything all better!

Your Sweetest Words

Speak kindly to everyone, but use your sweetest words for the people you see and spend time with every day— your mom and dad, your brother and sister, your teacher, your best friend across the street.

Also, make sure that the words that come out of your mouth are honest and true. Never say things that aren't true (unless you're playing pretend and making up a funny story, of course) because that could make someone feel sad. Sweet words make everyone glad!

Thank You Very Much!

"Thank you!" Say these words when people do nice things for you—when your aunt gives you a new stuffed animal, when your mom bakes chocolate chip cookies, when your brother picks up your toys for you.

When you say "thank you," other people want to do nice things for you. And you'll want to do nice things for them. And pretty soon *everyone* will be doing nice things for everyone else! Thank-you manners make the world a happy, happy place!

A Letter Is Even Better

Do you know what is even better than *saying* thank you? Giving someone a written thank-you note! Even if you don't know how to write yet, a thank-you picture is just as nice (maybe even better!).

Say Please!

If you need something, always add the words "please" or "May I?" to your request. Saying please—and then saying thank you when you are given what you asked for— is a sure way to get what you need.

I'm Very Sorry

When something goes wrong and you've hurt someone's feelings or broken something, you might want to cry or get really upset. It's all right to show how you feel by crying, but when the tears are through and you're feeling a little bit better, you can just say, "I'm sorry" or "Please excuse me." Then the other person will say, "I forgive you." A shared hug can make things happy again.

My Friendship Manners

SHARING AND CARING TOGETHER

One of the best things about getting bigger and growing up is making new friends. There are so many fun people to meet and play with! You can meet them at the park, in your neighborhood, at school, at church, in a playgroup—anywhere you go, you're sure to find a fun friend.

The Heart of Friendship

Have you ever heard of the Golden Rule? It's a little saying that tells you all you need to know about being a good friend and having good friendship manners:

Do unto others as you would have them do unto you.

The heart of having a good friendship is doing good things for each other.

Good friends always stick together and are there for each other.

Good friends always help each other.

Good friends always listen to each other.

Good friends always have fun playing together.

Fun and Games

When you're playing games with your friends, make sure you always follow the rules and tell the truth. Use nice words and don't make a big deal if you win or lose. What matters is that you do your very best, cheer for each other ("Good job!" "Way to go!"), and have a bunch of fun.

It's fun to run around with your friends, playing chase and tag and having races. But you should never throw things at people, call someone a name, or make unkind faces. These things can hurt people on the outside *and* on the inside. Remember that Golden Rule! Only do something to someone if you would want the very same thing done to you.

Sharing Is Caring

Good friends use the best kind of sharing manners with each other. You've probably heard someone say, "Sharing is caring." And that's true! Sharing is a way of saying, "I like you. You're a fun friend. Let's do this together!"

If you have a whole bunch of stickers or a great big stack of coloring books, it's nice to give some to your friend. You should check with a parent first, but your mom or dad will probably say that it's fine to give away some of your things—especially if your friend doesn't have as much as you have. And if you share with others, they will share with you!

Way to Play!

Sharing happens all the time when you play—even if you aren't playing indoors with toys! For instance, sometimes it takes a little while to figure out what to do. You want to climb trees, but your friend wants to build castles in the sandbox. What should you do?

It's not very fun to stand around and argue about it. It *is* fun to play. So share your creative ideas. Say, "Let's build castles until snack time. And then we can climb trees!"

My Playing Manners

HAVING AND BEING
A HAPPY GUEST

"Can you come over to play?" It's so much fun to invite a friend over. And it's just as much fun to spend the afternoon playing at a friend's house! Your very best manners can make playtime a lot of fun for everyone.

Welcome to My House!

Here's a great big word: *hospitality.* It sounds like a grown-up word, but it's actually kids who have the chance to show hospitality the most. After all, who has more play dates—you and your friends, or your parents and their friends? You do!

Hospitality is really quite simple. It just means that when you have friends over to your house, you do your best to help them feel welcome and special.

Come On In!

When your friend comes over to play, you should meet her at the door and say, "Hi, I'm glad you're here. Come in!"

Show her where to put her coat, tell her if she needs to take off her shoes or if she can leave them on, and let her know where she can put anything else she brought.

It's helpful to let your friend know where your bathroom is. You can let her know about any important rules you have in your house: "It's all right to pet the cats, but we can't let my sister's snake out of its cage."

Friends First

When you're using your playing manners, here's one super important thing to remember: Your guest (the friend who's over at your house) always goes first. Let her have the first choice of juice box or yogurt flavor. When you play a game, she gets the first turn. If there's just one pretty pink cup left, let her have it.

Something Special

Sometimes you and your friend both want to play with the very same toy. What should you do? Remember the little rule about letting your friend have the first choice. If she wants to wear your favorite princess dress-up gown, it's nice to let her.

If there is something that is really special to you that you don't want your friend to play with, you can ask your mom or dad to help you put it away before your friend comes over.

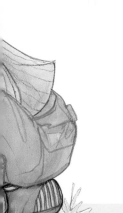

Happy to Be Here

When you're a guest, the number-one thing to remember is that it should be easy for your friend's family to have you around. Just be kind and helpful and remember your "magic" manners words, and you'll do just fine.

Before you go in the house, wipe your feet at the door. Then you can say, "Thanks for having me over to play!" Inside the house, make sure you keep your feet off the furniture (save climbing for trees and playground!) and always ask before you pick up anything that looks pretty or special.

Sometimes you might work on a big craft project—finger painting or cutting and pasting or stringing beads—that is a lot of fun but kind of messy. It's important to always help clean up before you go home.

Follow the Rules

It's really important to remember that in your friend's house, they might follow different rules. Some rules are the same everywhere you go. You should always, always wash your hands after going to the bathroom or before you eat something. But some things are probably different. Maybe you are allowed to eat food in your living room, but your friend's family only eats in the dining room or kitchen.

The last thing to do comes at the very end of your visit. Be sure to say a great big "thank you" to your friend and her family for having you over to play: "Thank you for inviting me over. I had a lot of fun. I'd love to play again!"

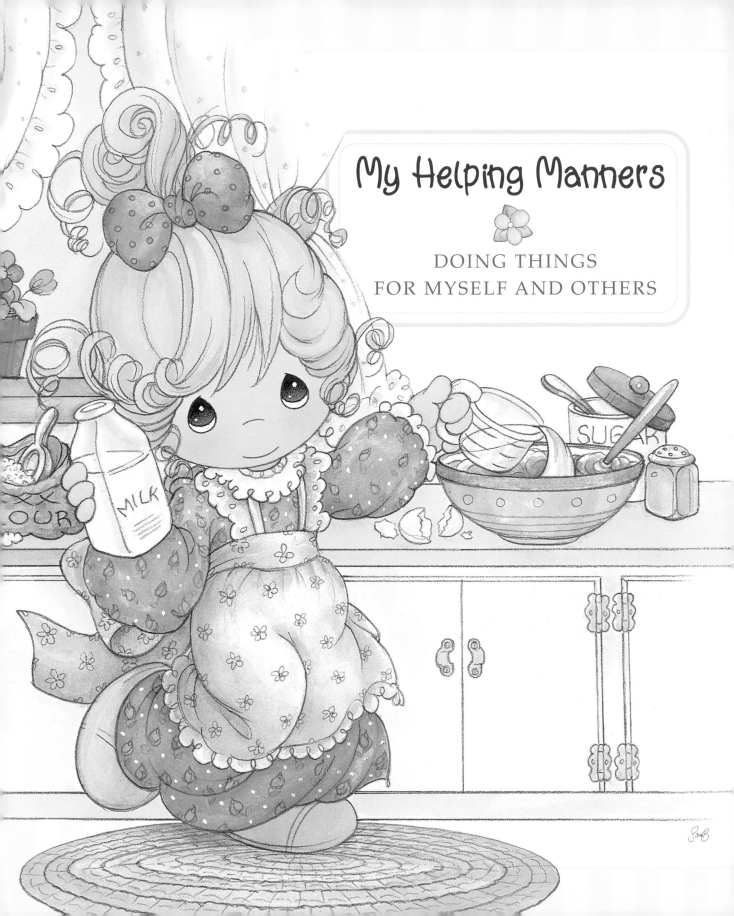

My Helping Manners

DOING THINGS FOR MYSELF AND OTHERS

Everyone likes a helping hand! Helping is a way of saying, "Here, let me do something for you. I care about you!" Or, "Let's do this together. The faster we finish, the sooner we can play!"

Helping at Home

Have you ever noticed that sometimes your house is really clean and neat—maybe when company is coming, or after your family has done some Saturday morning cleaning—but other times it can turn into a big mess?

You can do your best to help your family keep your house clean. It starts with always picking up after yourself. Put your books back on the bookshelf. Keep your crayons all together in a box or basket. Hang up your coat, and put your shoes on the shoe rack.

When you're doing your chores, it's fun to turn them into a game. See how quickly you can make your bed. Pretend you're a princess trapped in a castle tower who can only get out after she's finished clearing the dishes off the table. *Feed* your clean, folded clothes to your hungry dresser drawers.

May I Help You?

If you see that someone has dropped a toy or some money, pick it up for them. If your brother's job is to sweep the floor, hold the dustpan for him. If your teacher is handing out coloring sheets to the class, say, "May I help you do that?"

It's always good manners to help your friends and your little brothers or little sisters. Your neighbors and older people—like grandparents—also love it when you say, "Is there anything I can do to help?"

Help Yourself

As soon as you are able to, wash your face and brush your teeth. (You can have a parent help you finish up your teeth, but you can get them started.) After you get dressed in the morning, put away your pajamas very neatly. Learn how to tie your shoes, buckle your sandals, and brush your hair. The more you do for yourself, the less your mom or dad has to do for you. And the more time you both have to play paper dolls or read a story together!

My Obeying Manners

DOING THE
RIGHT THING AT
THE RIGHT TIME

"Yes, I will!"

"Okay, that sounds great!"

"Of course I can!"

These words are so sweet to hear. When you use your best obeying manners, you show respect—or caring and love—to your parents and the other grown-ups who help you—grandparents, teachers, and pastors.

Do It Right Away

When your mom or your teacher asks you to please do something, be sure to do it right away—with a great big smile. "I will" sounds so much sweeter than "I won't." And if they ask you to *stop* doing something, be sure to stop doing it right away, too!

If your parents tell you that you can't do something or have something—for example, you can't get out the finger paints right before your cousins come over, or you can't have a big bowl of ice cream right before you go to bed—it's best to just do what they say and go on with the next thing. Watch for your cousins' car, or pick out your favorite bedtime story. Be sure *not* to keep pestering your parents over and over: "*Please* can I get out the finger paints? Can I? Can I? Can I?" "Just *two* big scoops of ice cream? Maybe just *one?*"

Sleepytime

When the day is done and you're all worn out from playing and learning, it's time to go to bed. Sometimes it's hard to take a bath and brush your teeth and wind down for sleep, but bedtime can also mean special stories, gentle foot massages, or favorite bedtime songs.

Good night! Sleep tight!

Keeping Safe

Obeying keeps you safe. When you're in the car, you need to be buckled into your car seat in case the driver has to stop suddenly. When you're crossing the street, look both ways and hold hands with someone in case cars are going too fast. When you're playing ball outside, always ask a grown-up to get a ball that rolls into the street.

If you use your best obeying manners, you'll probably be able to start doing some things sooner. Maybe your dad will let you stand on a step stool to stir the soup. Or your mom will let you carefully wash the fancy water goblets. Or your grandpa will let you help in his woodshop if you obey his rules.

My Mealtime Manners

HAVING A HAPPY MEAL

Time to eat!

Sometimes that means a big breakfast of steaming hot pancakes with melting butter and maple syrup. Other times it's an outdoor picnic lunch of peanut butter sandwiches, carrots with dip, and slushy, ice-cold juice boxes. It may even be dinner out at your favorite pizza place.

Mealtimes are when we feed our bodies with food and our hearts with friendship. We can tell our dad about our day at the park or ask our mom a million questions about dinosaurs. We can try new foods and enjoy our old favorites.

Getting Ready

Go into the bathroom and wash your hands thoroughly. It's fun to sing "Happy Birthday" while you wash your hands—even if it's not your birthday—to make sure you've washed your hands long enough to get them nice and clean.

Mealtime manners start with a little dose of helping manners—setting the table. It's fun to set a pretty table, and you can start learning how to do it! Then go to the table and sit down with everyone else.

Many families say a blessing—a little prayer to give thanks for the food—and every family has their own way of doing this. You can hold hands, take turns saying the blessing, or even sing your blessing!

35

Time to Eat!

When you're ready to eat, place your napkin in your lap. If you're eating something really messy like spaghetti or tomato soup, you might need to also wear a bib.

Sit still in your chair and sit up straight with your elbows at your side (not on the table). Never rock back and forth in your chair or climb on the table. That could cause big spills—for the food *and* for you!

Table Talk

Everyone loves to talk at the table, but make sure you chew and swallow your food, *then* talk. Just pretend that your mouth is a door that automatically closes when you're chewing food.

Eat and drink quietly—no loud chomps or wild slurps. Take small bites and little sips. Use your utensils, not your fingers, to eat your food (unless you see your parents eating certain foods with their fingers).

Families have different rules about playing with your food. Some parents let their kids make mashed potato-and-broccoli forests. Some don't. If you're at someone else's house or if you have guests over for a meal, it's probably best not to play with your food.

Finishing Up

When you're done eating, you can nicely ask, "May I please be excused?"

Before you go play, it's always nice to help clear off your dishes, wipe up any crumbs or spills at your place, and carefully push in your chair.

There's just one more thing to do. Say a great big "thank you" to the person who made the meal!

My Partytime Manners

MAKING
THE MOST
OF FUN TIMES

Parties are fun! You get to dress up. You get to give—or receive—presents. You get to play games and have a wonderful time.

Parties Big and Small

Sometimes it's fun to have a tea party with just one or two best friends, or even with just your mom or grandma or sister. Other times your party might be a big birthday party or a gathering for your whole ballet class or Sunday school group.

You and your parents can make out the guest list and send out the party invitations. Pretty soon you'll find out who will be coming, and then very soon it will be time for the party to begin. Hurray!

It's My Party

When your friends come over to your house for a party, greet them at the door. If they bring you presents, say a big "thank you" and put the gifts aside until present-opening time.

Your mom or dad can help you explain what you're going to do and what you're going to play at the party. And even though this is your special party, you should never tell everyone what to do.

You can set a good example for the games by doing a good job of taking turns and by letting the youngest person at the party—maybe your little brother or sister—go first. (Sometimes, if it's your birthday, you might get to go first!) Be happy for the kids who win games. Better yet, before the party you can help your parents plan some games where everyone wins!

A Great Gift-Getter

Be sure to say out loud who the gift is from, read any card (it's fun to pass the cards around), and then open the present. You can hold it up for everyone to see and then say a great big "thank you" and something really nice about the present: "I love purple!" "This is such a cute stuffed bunny!" "Ooohhh! Look at this fancy necklace!"

Being a Partygoer

When you're going to someone else's party, wear your best party clothes (unless it's a swim party or gymnastics party) and bring along a gift if it's a birthday party.

When you get to the party, first say hello or "happy birthday" to the guest of honor. Then you can give her your gift and say hello to anyone else you know. You can also meet some new friends!

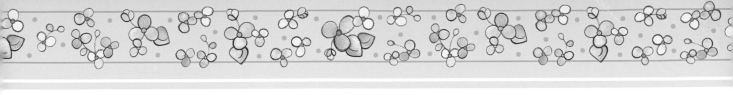

Join in the Fun

Some parties have a lot of games and activities. Others have mostly free playtime. Either way, just join in the fun! If you don't know the rules of a game or you're not sure what to do, just ask a grown-up.

Sometimes it's hard to watch one child open present after present when there's nothing for you. But remember that when your birthday comes, you will have lots of gifts, too!

Thanks for Having Me!

When it's time to leave the party, be sure to find your host and her parents and thank them: "Thanks so much! I really had a nice time! Happy birthday!"

My Growing-Up Manners

EVERY DAY I LEARN
NEW THINGS

Every day you're learning new things—how to skip, how to play games, maybe even how to read and write!

As you grow up, you keep learning new manners. But they're easy to learn if you just remember the Golden Rule: Do unto others as you would have them do unto you.

Let's Talk About It

Way back at the beginning of this book, you learned how to talk to new people and how to use words that are nice and polite. It's always important to be friendly to people, but it's also important to be safe. It's probably not the best idea to walk up to a bigger kid or a grown-up you don't know and start talking to him or her. It's a better idea to get your parent and to talk to the person together.

45

Telephone Talk

Are you learning how to answer the telephone? That's really fun! Using your nicest manners can help make telephone talk a breeze.

When the phone rings, you can say, "Hello" and who you are. Use your polite words—"please" and "thank you"—and put a big smile on your face.

If the telephone call is for someone else, all you need to do is politely ask the person on the phone to wait while you get the other person: "One moment, please. I'll go get my dad."

If you have a play phone, you can practice having pretend telephone conversations. Or just use a banana or a wooden block as your telephone!

Everyone Plays!

Always include everyone who wants to play! It's not nice to say, "I'm only playing with her today," or "Girls only on the slide." Everyone deserves a chance at playtime and friendship!

Always Ask

If you see something that looks neat but it doesn't belong to you—a shiny red shovel, a brightly colored beach ball, a pretty necklace—ask for permission before you play with it.

If the other person says yes, great! You can play with the item. Be sure to be careful with it! If they say no, that's okay. Just find something else to do.

Oopsie-Daisy!

Even though you try your best to do the right thing, sometimes things go wrong. You hurt someone's feelings. You accidentally break someone's toy. You leave a mess for someone else to pick up. What should you do then?

The best thing to do is to say a great big "I'm sorry" that comes straight from your heart. Then do something to make it better. Draw a picture for your friend whose feelings were hurt. Help fix your sister's toy. Help out around the house to make up for the mess you made.

In any situation, just remember to be kind and considerate of others, and your good manners will follow right along.

You're off to a terrific start!